MW00903372

Mary Blocksma

WHAT'S IN THE WOODS?

A Michigan Treasure Hunt

Art and Text by Mary Blocksma

Beaver Island Arts

What's in the Woods?
A Michigan Treasure Hunt
First Edition

To request permission for reprints and excerpts, or to purchase prints, note cards, original art, or educational support material, please contact the publisher:

Beaver Island Arts
P.O. Box 40
Bay City, MI 48707-0040
989-894-5925
http://beaverislandarts.com

Printed in the United States of America
10 9 8 7 6 5 4 3 2 1

ISBN-13 978-09708575-3-8

Cataloging Data provided by Mary Blocksma, M.L.S.:

Blocksma, Mary.
What's in the woods? : a Michigan treasure hunt/ art and text by Mary Blocksma.
p. cm.
Includes index.
SUMMARY : Introduction to natural wonders through the seasons in Michigan woods shows the difference between seed-eating and insect-eating birds, tells how to find and identify common trees, how to avoid dangerous plant and animal species, and much more.
Audience: Ages 6-12
ISBN-13 978-09708575-3-8

1. Zoology--Nomenclature (Popular)--Juvenile literature. 2. Plant names, Popular--Juvenile literature. 3. Natural history--Michigan--Juvenile literature. [1. Animals. 2. Vocabulary. 3. Plant names, popular. 4. Natural history.] I. Title

508.774

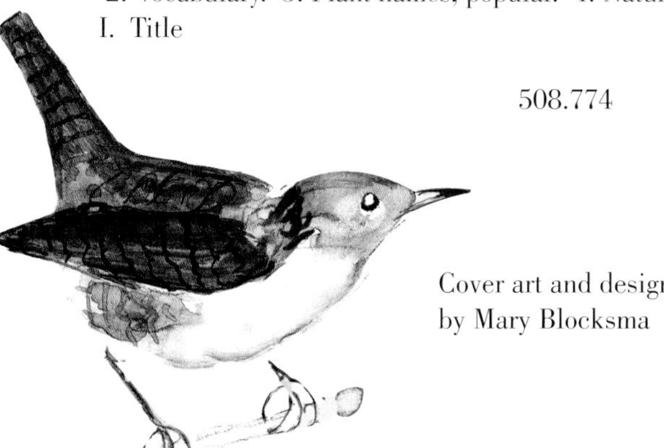

Cover art and design
by Mary Blocksma

Table of Contents

Wild Turkeys Inside front cover
You Can Do It! 4
Big Loud Birds 6
Small Winter Seed-Eaters 8
Three Woodpeckers 10
Raptors by Day and by Night 12
Big Low-Flying Birds 14
Aerial Acrobats 15
Small Mammals by Day and by Night 16
Big Mammals 18
Easy Evergreens 19
Enter Spring 22
Seven Spring Wildflowers 24
Ten Easy Trees 26
Which Maple? 28
Which Oak? 29
Small Flitting Bug-Eaters 30
Loud Summer Birds 31
Six Summer Wildflowers 32
Opposite-Leaf Shrubs 34
Alternate-Leaf Shrubs 35
Butterflies by Day 36
Moths at Night 37
Odd Green Plants 38
Fern Frills 39
Mushrooms All Year 40
Bugs That Bite or Sting 42
Bugs That Don't 43
Brambles Scratch! 44
These Berries Don't! 45
Topical Index 46
Books by Mary Blocksma 48
Treasure Hunt Inside back cover

You Can Do This!

Binoculars

Use a pair of binoculars to bring far-off birds, butterflies—even tree leaves—close enough to identify. A small, light pair won't feel too heavy around your neck.

Binocular art by Robin Wilt, University of Michigan Press. Used with permission

If you can recognize our most common plants and wildlife, you will know much of what you see in Michigan woods. Nearly everyone in Michigan lives close to the woods—the U.S. Forest Service reports that more than half of the state is forested. Get to know the woods near you, or adventure to one of Michigan's state and national parks and forests.

Remember—*What's in the Woods?* is a treasure hunt, a way to begin. To find everything, you will need to explore more than one woodlot or forest, in more than one season. Soon you will know more species in our forests than most people do. Learn to identify everything in this book to be well on your way to becoming an amateur naturalist.

What's in the Woods? is arranged loosely by season. See how many of the 145 species in this book can you find!

Take Care of Yourself.

Although Michigan woods are rarely dangerous, it's wise to be cautious, especially if you are unfamiliar with a place you are exploring.

• Don't put anything in your mouth unless you or someone you are with knows for certain that it is safe.

• If you are in a park, try to get a trail map, so you know where you are.

• Good things to take in a daypack: binoculars, bottle of water, sunscreen, insect repellent, a loud whistle or siren (in case you get lost), and a compass (if you know how to use one).

• Do not approach wild animals, especially when they are with their young. Bear and moose are known to fiercely protect their cubs and calves.

Take Care of the Woods.

Getting to know what's what in the woods is a good way to take care of Michigan's natural environments. You can also follow these tips:

• Pack out all your trash.

• Pack out other people's trash.

• Don't feed the animals.

• Keep pets on a leash.

• Follow park rules.

• Do not disturb birds or animals.

• Do not pick or cut any plant unless you know that it isn't one of Michigan's endangered or threatened species. Many of Michigan's plants are protected by law.

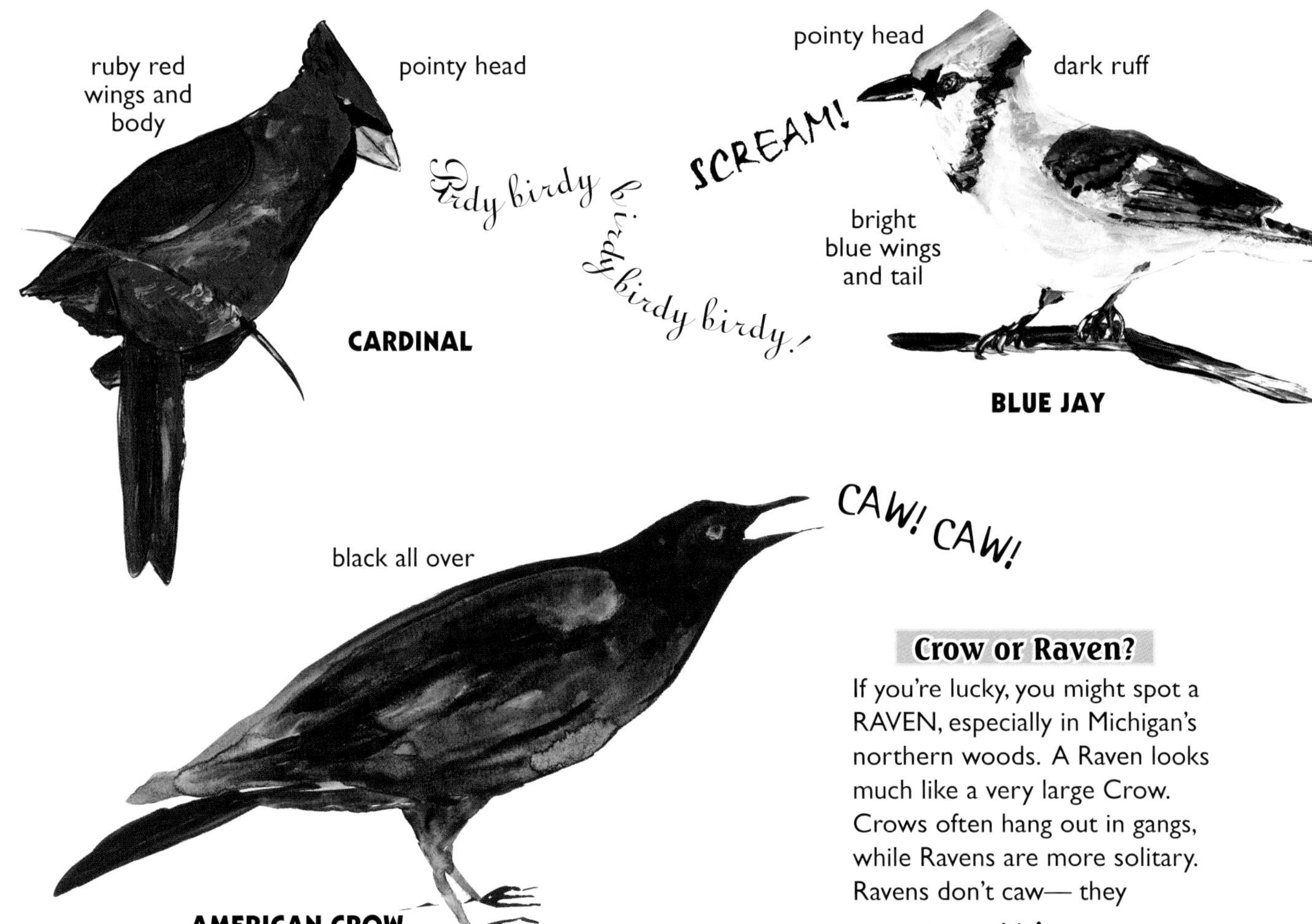
ruby red wings and body
pointy head
CARDINAL
Birdy birdy birdy birdy birdy birdy!
SCREAM!
pointy head
dark ruff
bright blue wings and tail
BLUE JAY
CAW! CAW!
black all over
AMERICAN CROW

Crow or Raven?

If you're lucky, you might spot a RAVEN, especially in Michigan's northern woods. A Raven looks much like a very large Crow. Crows often hang out in gangs, while Ravens are more solitary. Ravens don't caw— they

CROAK!

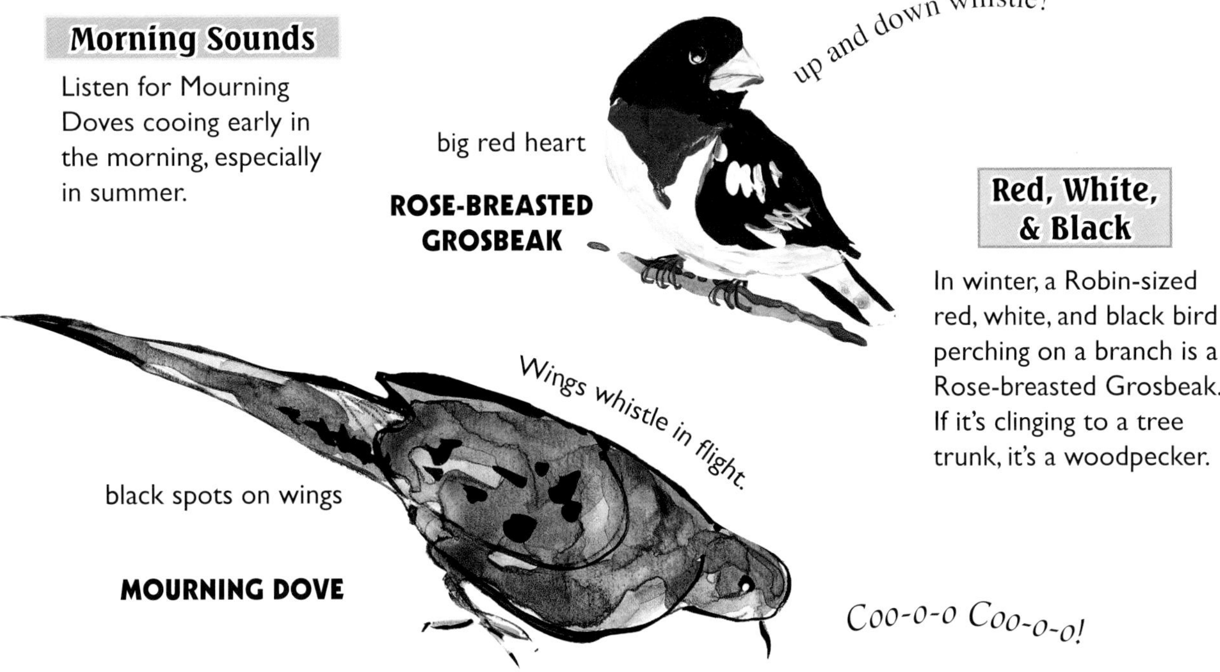

Morning Sounds
Listen for Mourning Doves cooing early in the morning, especially in summer.
big red heart
ROSE-BREASTED GROSBEAK
up and down whistle!
Red, White, & Black
In winter, a Robin-sized red, white, and black bird perching on a branch is a Rose-breasted Grosbeak. If it's clinging to a tree trunk, it's a woodpecker.
Wings whistle in flight.
black spots on wings
MOURNING DOVE
Coo-o-o Coo-o-o!

Big Loud Birds

To begin treasure-hunting in the Michigan woods, start listening. Robin-sized or bigger, these birds are especially easy to spot when the trees are leafless in winter or early spring. You can lure them to your yard with sunflower seeds in a birdfeeder.

Small Winter Seed-Eaters

You'll probably see these small birds if you fill bird feeders with sunflower and thistle seeds. The tiny finches are especially fond of thistle seeds. At first it's hard to tell little birds apart, but if you follow the clues, you'll soon know what to look for.

Little Brown Birds

In Michigan, the little brown bird that you see in winter is probably a House Sparrow or a House Finch. Little brown birds are harder to tell apart the rest of the year, when there are more kinds.

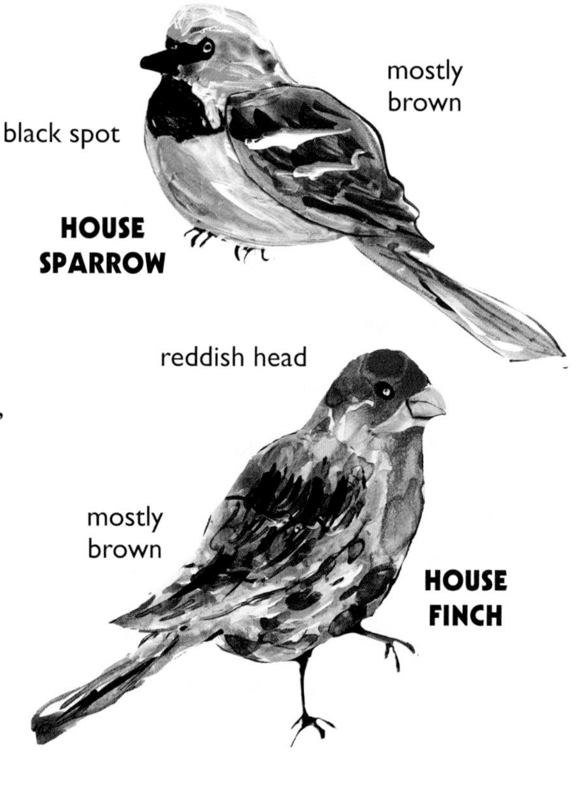
black spot
mostly brown
HOUSE SPARROW
reddish head
mostly brown
HOUSE FINCH

House Sparrows and House Finches hang out near houses, often in big groups.

pointy head
Titmice are loners.
Pe-ter!
Pe-ter!
Pe-ter!
TUFTED TITMOUSE

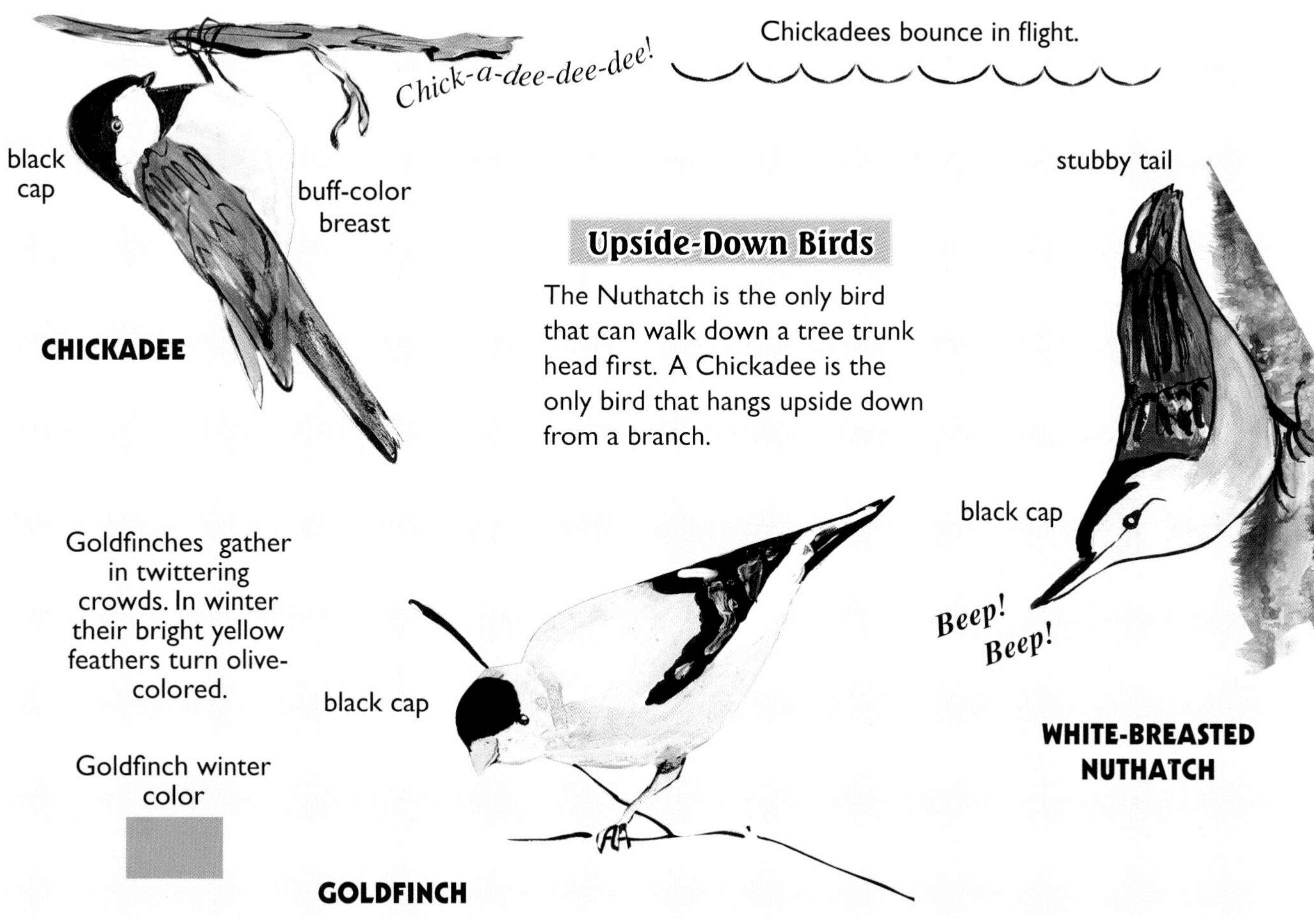
Chickadees bounce in flight.
Chick-a-dee-dee-dee!
black cap
buff-color breast
CHICKADEE
stubby tail
black cap
Beep! Beep!
WHITE-BREASTED NUTHATCH
black cap
GOLDFINCH
Goldfinch winter color

Upside-Down Birds

The Nuthatch is the only bird that can walk down a tree trunk head first. A Chickadee is the only bird that hangs upside down from a branch.

Goldfinches gather in twittering crowds. In winter their bright yellow feathers turn olive-colored.

red
spot
red
spot
DOWNY
WOODPECKER
HAIRY
WOODPECKER

Almost Twins

The Downy Woodpecker is smaller than the Hairy Woodpecker, but the two birds are hard to tell apart unless seen together.

Suet Clue

It's common to see Downy and Hairy Woodpeckers clinging to a hunk of suet as well as to the trunks of trees. Buy suet at your grocery store and hang it outside your house.

Three Woodpeckers and a Junco

A bright flash of black, white, and red, especially in winter, is likely some kind of woodpecker. Learn to recognize woodpeckers by their screams, loud tapping, and loopy flight patterns.

red head
RED-HEADED WOODPECKER

Tell a woodpecker in the air by its loopy flight pattern.

White-edged tail fans out in flight.
JUNCO

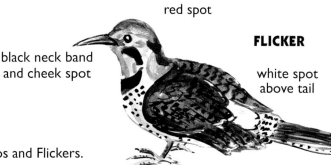

red spot

FLICKER

black neck band and cheek spot

white spot above tail

Look on the ground for feeding Juncos and Flickers.

RED-TAILED HAWK
speckled chest band
reddish tail

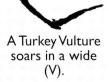

A Turkey Vulture soars in a wide (V).

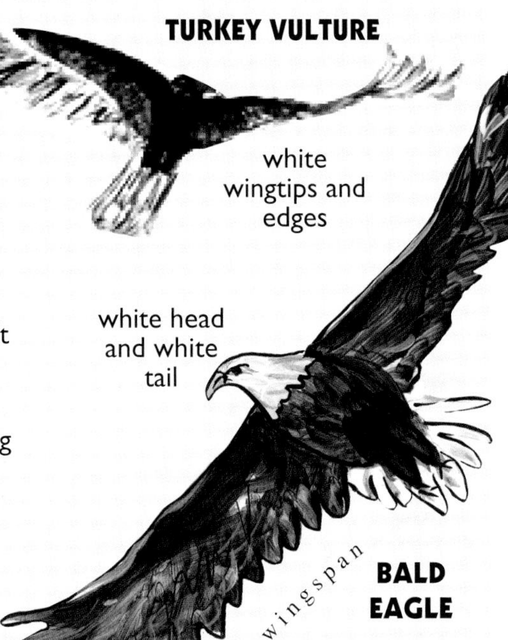
TURKEY VULTURE
white wingtips and edges
white head and white tail
6-foot wingspan
BALD EAGLE

Wing Watch

See that big bird high overhead? If its wings don't move much and form a wide, tilting V, it's a Turkey Vulture. A Bald Eagle's long narrow wings flap slowly and steadily. Hawks often alternate flapping and flat-winged soaring.

Raptors by Day...

Meat-eating birds—like hawks, eagles, vultures, and owls—are called ***raptors.*** Both big and small raptors are equipped with strong, sharp claws and beaks. Watch for them as they hunt, soaring the skies or perching on high bare branches out in the open.

...Raptors at Night

Owls fly silently on special, soft feathers. An owl can sometimes be spotted during the day being harrassed by a gang of noisy crows. Crows hate owls and try to chase them away. At night, listen for eerie owl calls, but remember—not all owls HOOT. A Snowy Owl can sound like a dog and the 6-inch Screech Owl often neighs like a horse!

BARK! BARK!
H-HOO-HOO-HOO!
N-e-i-g-h-h-h-h-h!
T-r-r-r-r-i-i-l-l!
SNOWY OWL
GREAT HORNED OWL
EASTERN SCREECH OWL

Big Low-Flying Birds

You can often get a good look at these big birds—none flies very high or for very long. If you surprise one in the brush, its whirring wings may startle you. Grouse and pheasants are often alone, but Wild Turkeys—especially females—usually wander the woods in big, gobbling groups.

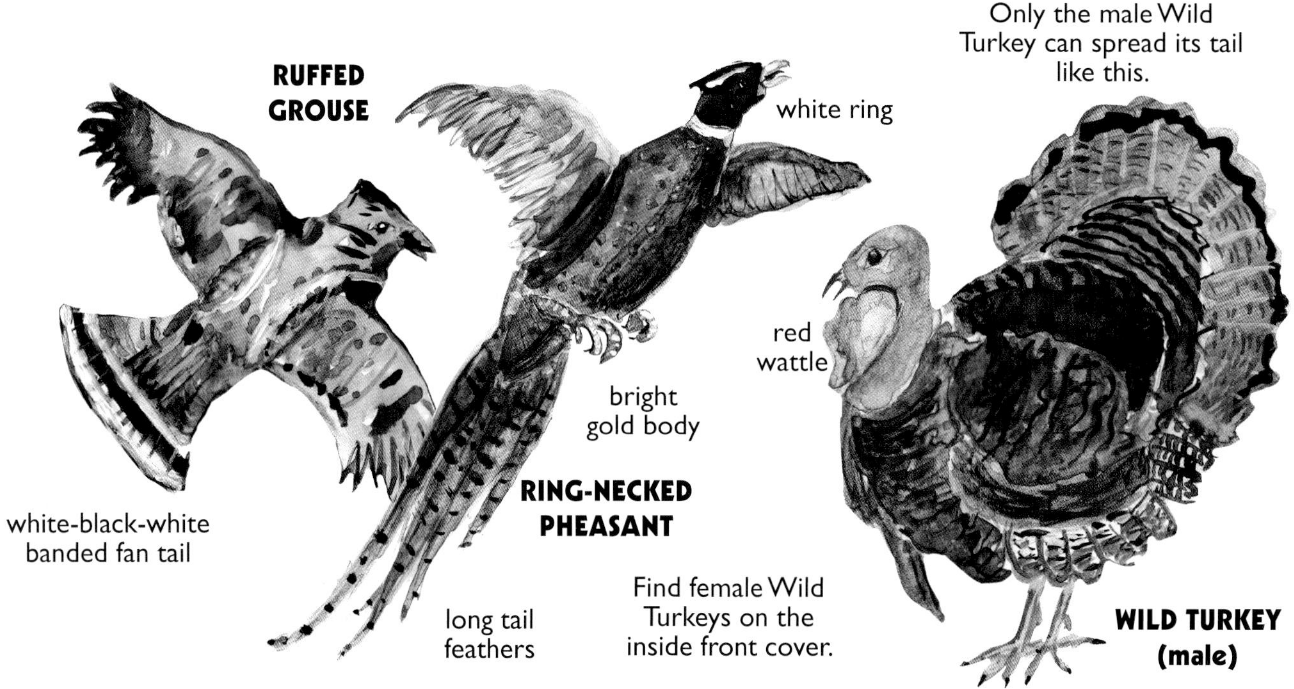
Only the male Wild Turkey can spread its tail like this.
RUFFED GROUSE
white ring
red wattle
bright gold body
RING-NECKED PHEASANT
white-black-white banded fan tail
long tail feathers
Find female Wild Turkeys on the inside front cover.
WILD TURKEY (male)

bushy tail
mostly gray or black

GRAY SQUIRREL

Squirrel or Chipmunk?

Chipmunks like to hide beneath and behind logs near their underground homes. Squirrels live in leafy nests high in tree branches and race and chase in the treetops as well as on the ground. Watch them raid your bird feeder!

Black, Gray, or Red Squirrel?

A Gray Squirrel may have gray or black fur—both colors can be in the same litter. The little Red Squirrel looks a lot like a chipmunk without stripes, but only chipmunks have stripes around their eyes.

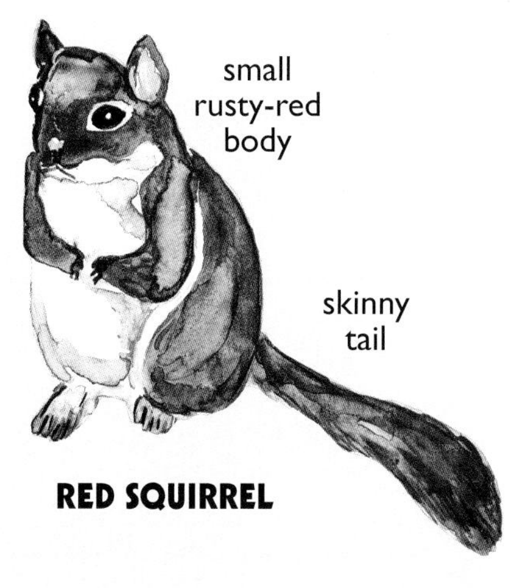
small rusty-red body
skinny tail

RED SQUIRREL

black-banded white stripe on each side
white stripes above & below the eyes

EASTERN CHIPMUNK

Small Animals by Day...

It's not polite to get too close to these animals, although probably they will flee if you do. Watch out!—a Porcupine's sharp quills can cause pain, and an upset Skunk (also a night creature) may spray a horrible STINK.

sharp quilled body

PORCUPINE

wide white stripe on each side
Watch out if this tail goes up—phew!
SKUNK

Rabbit or Hare?

The small brown rabbit you see in lower Michigan is likely a Cottontail. In northern Michigan, you might see the larger Snowshoe Hare. In spring and fall, a Snowshoe Hare's fur often shows odd puzzle-like patterns as the color of its coat changes.

EASTERN COTTONTAIL

shorter legs

SNOWSHOE HARE (in summer)

extra-long ears

extra-long legs

SNOWSHOE HARE (in winter)

big snowshoe feet

FLYING SQUIRREL
Although the Flying Squirrel doesn't really fly, flaps between its front and back legs let it glide from branch to branch.
BROWN BAT
Look for the jagged paths of bats!
A bat eats thousands of pesky mosquitos.
...and at Night
Sometimes see babies on mama's back.
OPOSSUM
long naked tail
RACCOON
black mask
ringed tail
Raccoons often get into trash cans.

Big Mammals

Reddish or brown coats help hide these big animals in summer and fall, but they're easy to see against winter snow. You might hear far-away Foxes and Coyotes, but White-tailed Deer bark only when startled. Moose live mostly in the northern parts of the state.

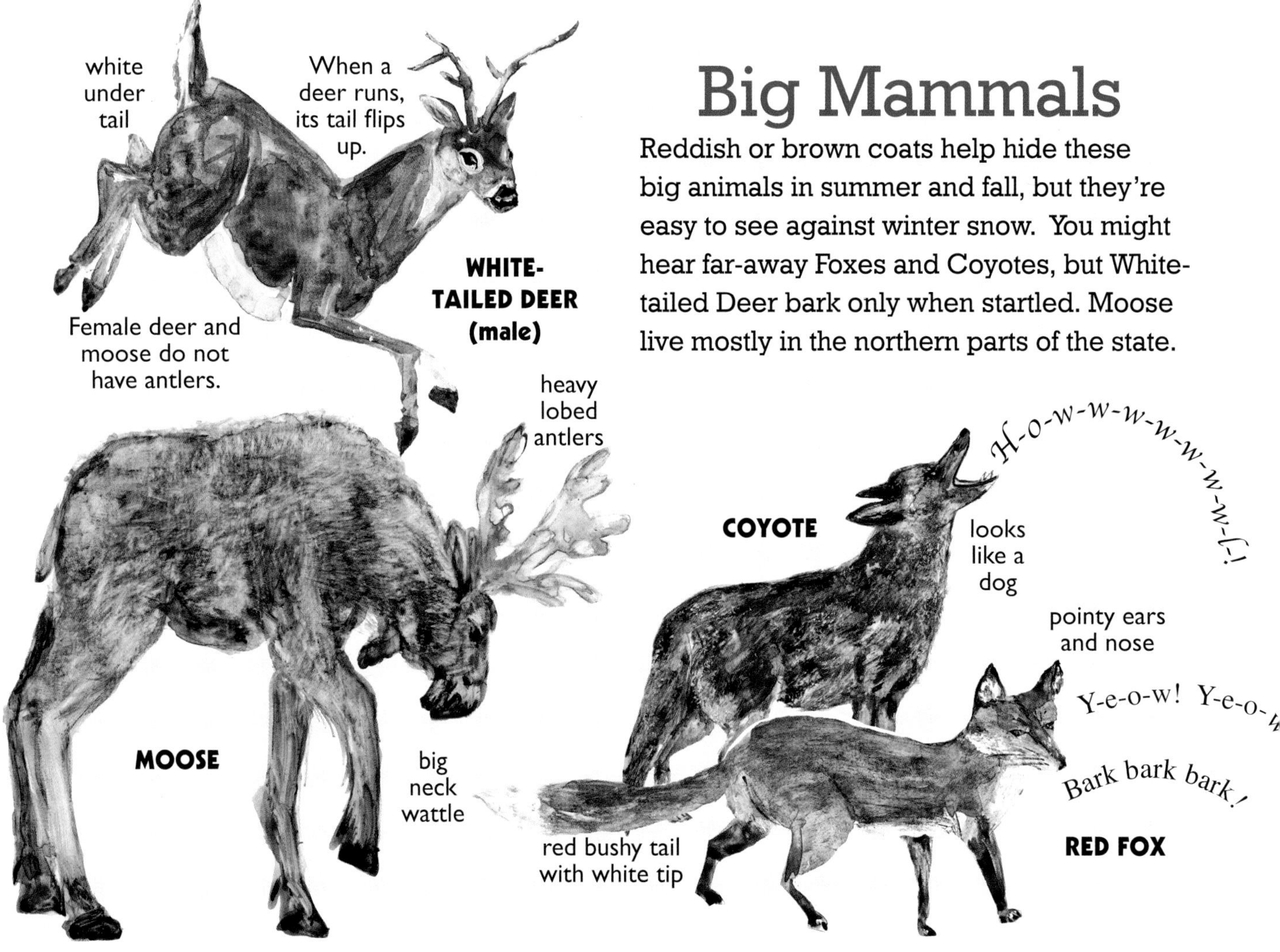
white
under
tail
When a
deer runs,
its tail flips
up.
WHITE-
TAILED DEER
(male)
Female deer and
moose do not
have antlers.
heavy
lobed
antlers
MOOSE
big
neck
wattle
H-o-w-w-w-w-w-w-w-w-l-!
COYOTE
looks
like a
dog
pointy ears
and nose
Y-e-o-w! Y-e-o-w
Bark bark bark!
RED FOX
red bushy tail
with white tip

Ten Easy Evergreens

Michigan evergreens aren't hard to identify—just divide them into three groups: 1) needles in bunches (this page), 2) needles not in bunches (page 20), or 3) scales (page 21).

5 long needles per bunch

WHITE PINE

long cone

2 long needles per bunch

rounded cone

RED PINE

Needles in Bunches

Many people call any evergreen tree a pine, but it's only a pine if its needles grow in bunches. In Michigan, it's likely to be one of these three native pines.

small cones cling to branch in pairs
JACK PINE
2 short needles per bunch

Needles NOT in Bunches

If an evergreen tree's needles grow right out of its stems and branches, and not in bunches, it is probably a cedar, hemlock, or a spruce. How easy is that?

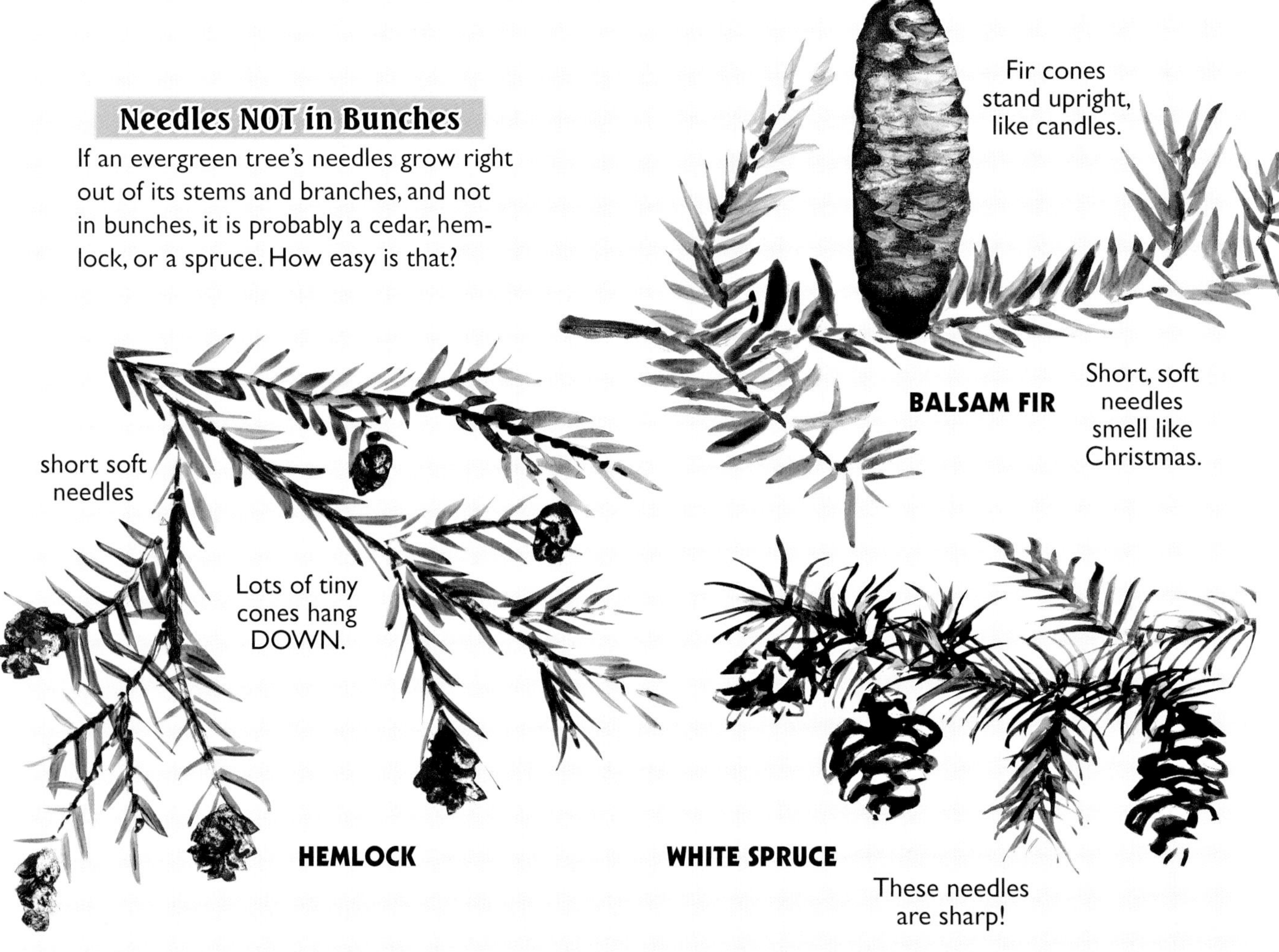
Fir cones stand upright, like candles.
BALSAM FIR
Short, soft needles smell like Christmas.
short soft needles
Lots of tiny cones hang DOWN.
HEMLOCK
WHITE SPRUCE
These needles are sharp!

Lots of tiny
cones stand UP
or cluster.
NORTHERN
WHITE CEDAR

Scaly Evergreens

Some Michigan evergreens have scales instead of needles. Tall Northern White Cedars grow in the northern half of the state. Red Cedars are flame-shaped and about the size of Christmas trees. See them often along the highway.

flame-shaped
medium-sized
tree
rusty-looking
foliage
RED CEDAR

soft sprays

That Odd Tamarack

A Tamarack looks like an evergreen in summer, but it loses its sprays of short needle-like leaves in the fall. Look for Tamaracks (also called Larches) in swampy places, especially up north.

Enter Spring!

In spring, many creatures, including *reptiles* (snakes and turtles) and *amphibians* (frogs, toads, and salamanders) are just waking up. They were *hibernating* (sleeping) through the cold months. Robins, however, have just flown in from the South.

BUMBLEBEE QUEEN
big buzzy bee in early spring

Z-Z-Z-Z-Z-Z-Z-Z-Z-Z-Z-Z-Z-Z-Z-Z-Z-Z-Z

Michigan's only kind of bear

BLACK BEAR

white ring around eye

orange-red breast

AMERICAN ROBIN

A Woodchuck often sits up like this.

dark brown all over

WOODCHUCK

Afraid of Snakes?

Michigan is home to only one poisonous snake—the Eastern Massasauga Rattlesnake—and it is rarely seen. Be kind to our snakes, turtles, and toads. Many are becoming scarce.

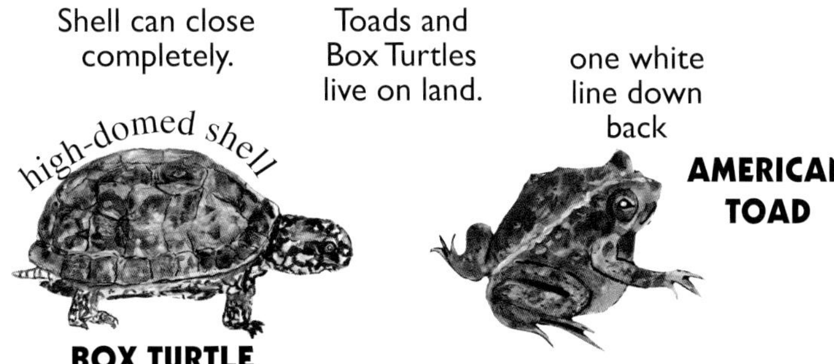
Shell can close completely.
Toads and Box Turtles live on land.
one white line down back
high-domed shell
AMERICAN TOAD
BOX TURTLE

Reptile or Amphibian?

Amphibians [am-FIB-i-ans] are four-legged animals that can live in water and on land. Reptiles [REP-tiles] are scaly animals with backbones. Not all reptiles have legs.

Look under logs for salamanders.

bright red stripe down back

RED-BACKED SALAMANDER

Danger! Heart-shaped head!

EASTERN MASSASAUGA RATTLESNAKE

rattles

Michigan's only poisonous snake

lengthwise red or yellow stripes

GARTER SNAKE

big spots like a cow

MILK SNAKE

Seven Spring Wildflowers

Don't pick the Trillium. It's a protected Michigan wildflower.
3 petals
butterfly-shaped blossoms
5 petals
3 sepals
smooth edges
2 long slim leaves, like wings
3 leaves
TRILLIUM
frilly leaves
SPRING BEAUTY
DUTCHMAN'S BREECHES

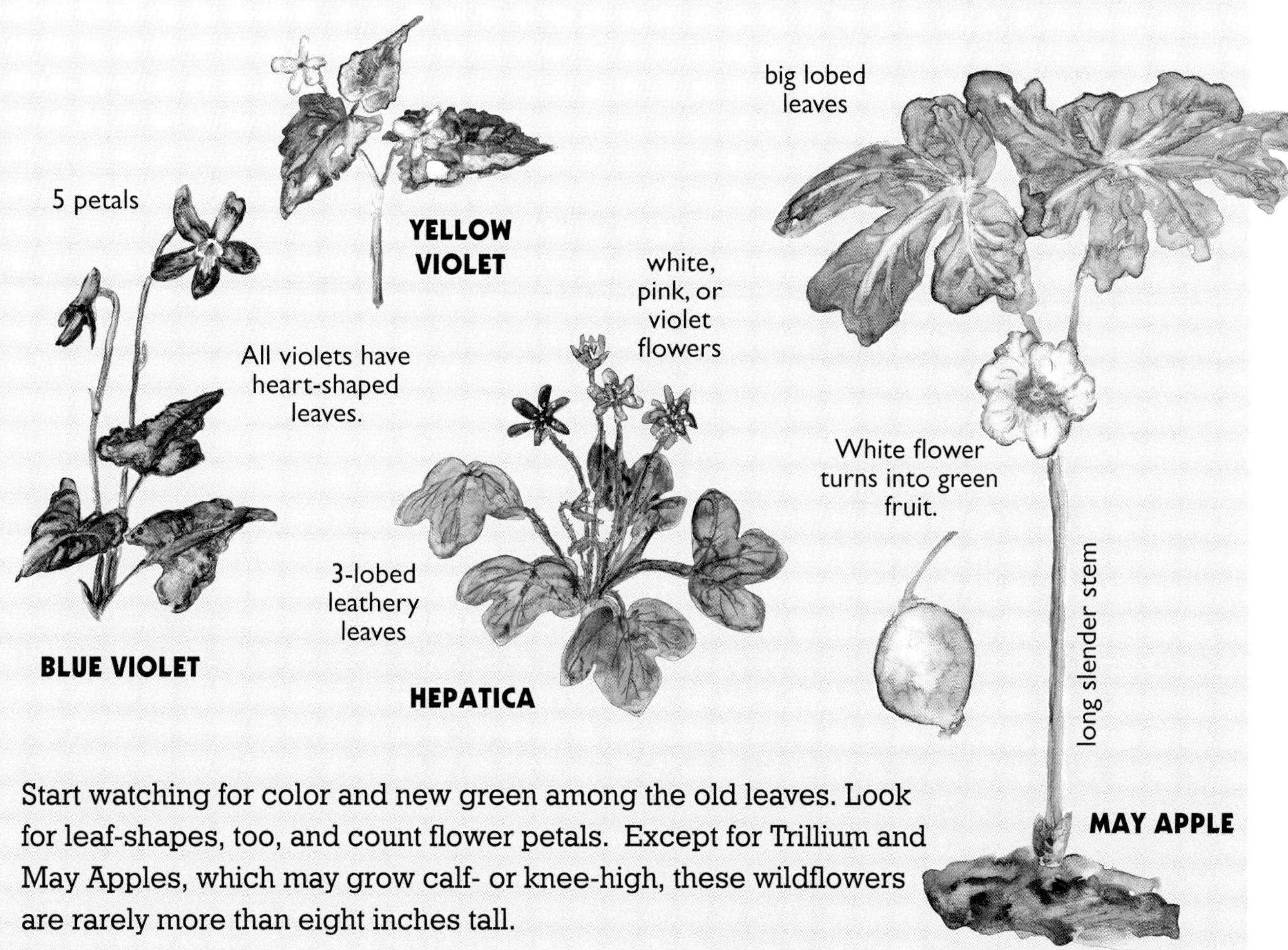
big lobed
leaves
5 petals
YELLOW
VIOLET
white,
pink, or
violet
flowers
All violets have
heart-shaped
leaves.
White flower
turns into green
fruit.
long slender stem
3-lobed
leathery
leaves
BLUE VIOLET
HEPATICA
MAY APPLE

Start watching for color and new green among the old leaves. Look for leaf-shapes, too, and count flower petals. Except for Trillium and May Apples, which may grow calf- or knee-high, these wildflowers are rarely more than eight inches tall.

Ten Easy Trees

At last—leaves! Most people give up at the sight of all that green, but there are many easy clues. When you can identify these trees, plus the oaks and maples on the next two pages, you'll know most of the broad-leaved trees in Michigan woods.

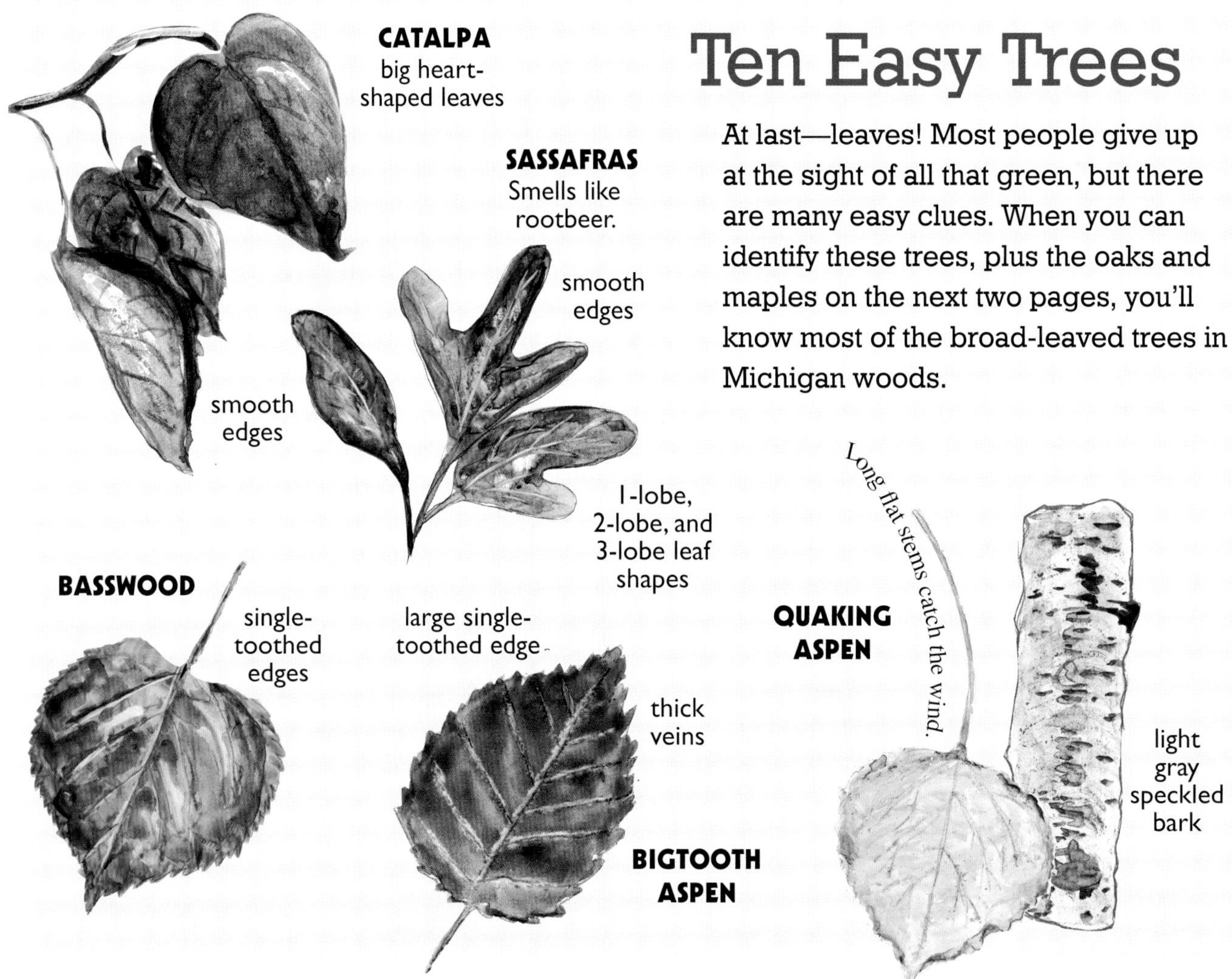
CATALPA
big heart-shaped leaves
smooth edges
SASSAFRAS
Smells like rootbeer.
smooth edges
1-lobe, 2-lobe, and 3-lobe leaf shapes
BASSWOOD
single-toothed edges
large single-toothed edge
thick veins
BIGTOOTH ASPEN
QUAKING ASPEN
Long flat stems catch the wind.
light gray speckled bark

Leaf Edges

After you notice a leaf's shape, check out its edge: Is it smooth, single-toothed, double-toothed, saw-toothed, or something unusual?

Odd Trunks

For some trees, the unusual color or feel of the trunk or bark is the best clue.

Most willows have long narrow leaves.

WILLOW

peeling white bark with dark lines

PAPER BIRCH

shaggy, shingle-like bark

HOP HORNBEAM

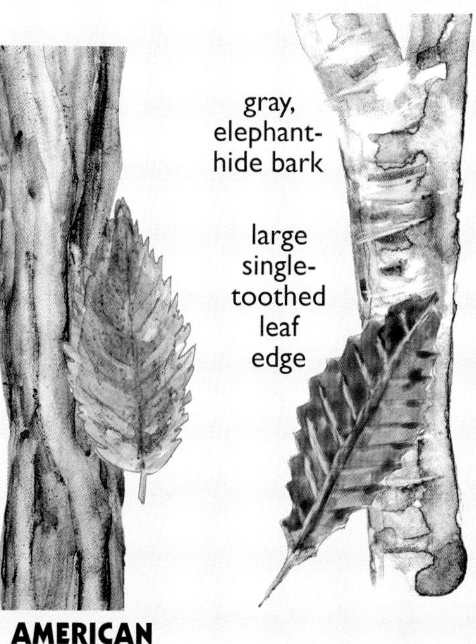
smooth, oddly muscular-looking trunk
gray, elephant-hide bark
large single-toothed leaf edge

AMERICAN HORNBEAM

BEECH

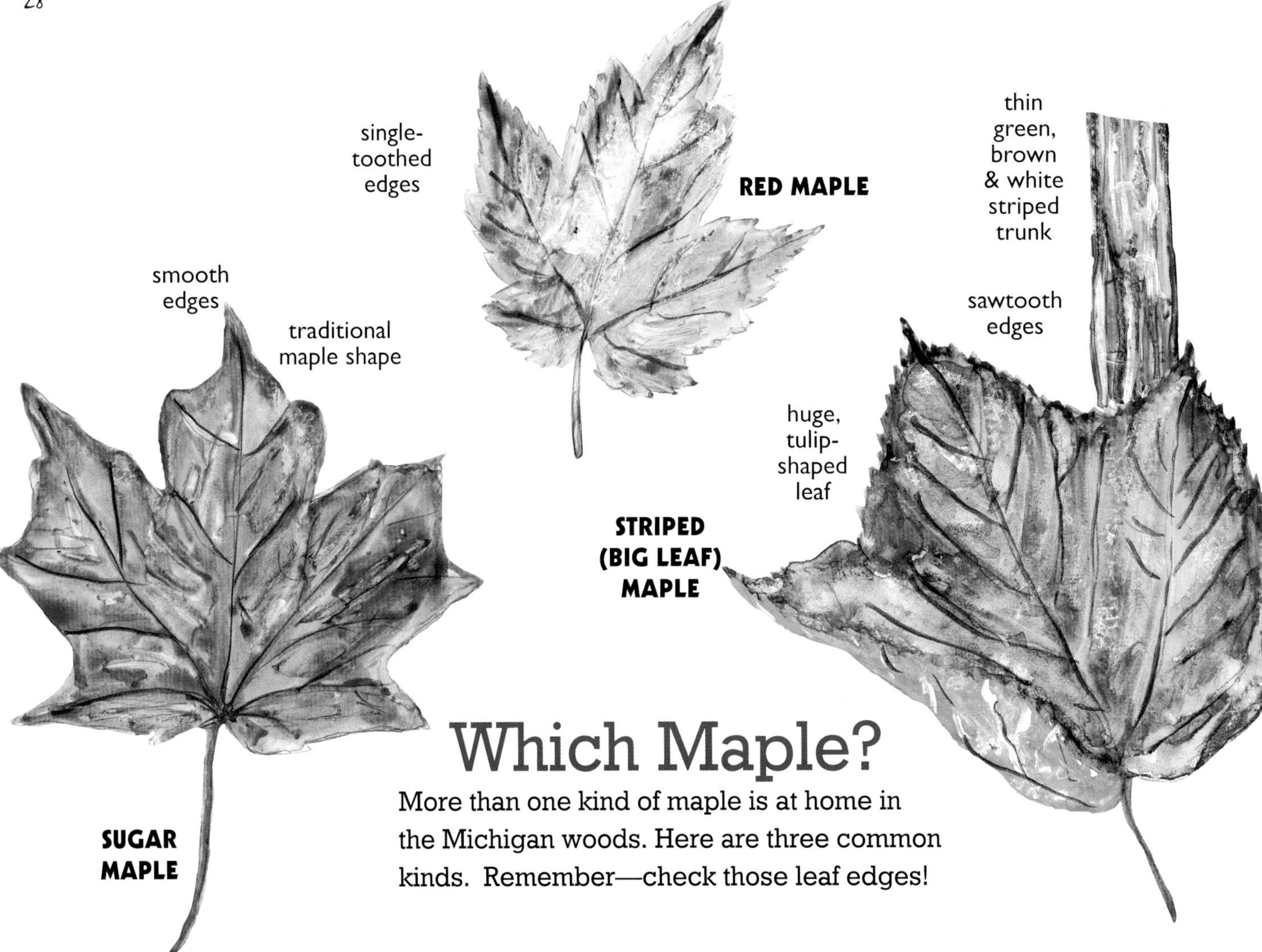
single-
toothed
edges
RED MAPLE
thin
green,
brown
& white
striped
trunk
smooth
edges
traditional
maple shape
sawtooth
edges
huge,
tulip-
shaped
leaf
STRIPED
(BIG LEAF)
MAPLE
SUGAR
MAPLE

Which Maple?

More than one kind of maple is at home in the Michigan woods. Here are three common kinds. Remember—check those leaf edges!

Pairs or Alternates?

Tree leaves either grow opposite each other, in pairs, or alternate up the stem or branch.

Maple leaves are opposite. Even the branches grow in pairs.

Oak leaves are alternate, staggered up the stem. Even the branches are staggered.

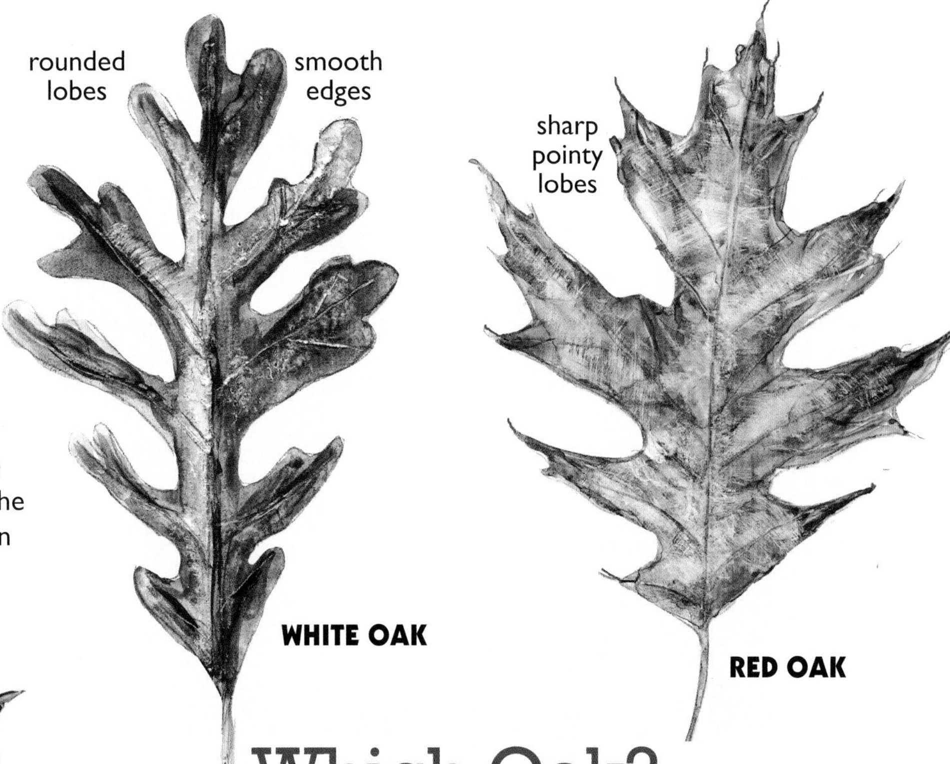
rounded lobes
smooth edges
sharp pointy lobes
WHITE OAK
RED OAK

Which Oak?

The many look-alike oak species often frustrate amateur naturalists, but oaks do fall into two easy-to-identify groups: A White Oak has leaves with rounded lobes, while a Red Oak has leaves with sharp angles.

Small Flitting Bug-Eaters

The bugs are back, and so are the bug-eating birds that flew south for the winter. Birds sing loudly at this time year to attract mates, but these small birds are hard to tell apart and rarely stay still for long. For now, just look for one bird in each of these insect-eating group: swallows, wrens, and warblers.

Wrens have a flicking, sticking-up tail.

HOUSE WREN

Wrens warble and twitter loud and long!

Swallows dart through the air like bats.

Swallows have forked tails.

TREE SWALLOW

Warblers have thin pointed beaks.

no black cap

red speckles on yellow breast

YELLOW WARBLER

Loud Summer Birds

You can often hear or see these robin-sized summer birds. Only the Wood Thrush is shy, but listen for its magical chiming song at dusk.

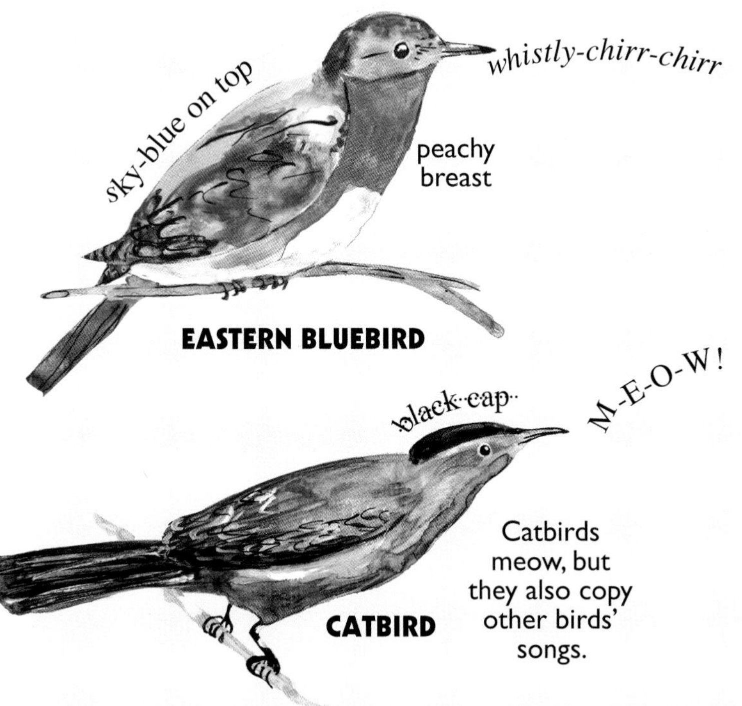
sky-blue on top
whistly-chirr-chirr
peachy breast
EASTERN BLUEBIRD
black cap
M-E-O-W!
Catbirds meow, but they also copy other birds' songs.
CATBIRD

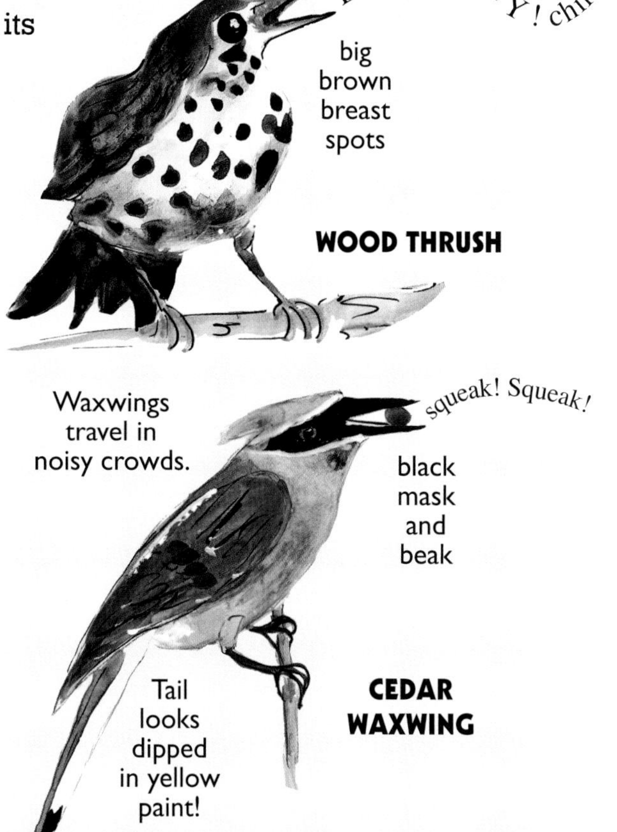
E-O-L-A-Y! chirr!
big brown breast spots
WOOD THRUSH
Waxwings travel in noisy crowds.
squeak! Squeak!
black mask and beak
Tail looks dipped in yellow paint!
CEDAR WAXWING

Six Summer Wildflowers

Blossom color is usually the first step in identifying a wildflower, but the best clue may be the shape of the blossom, stem, or leaf. All the wildflowers on this page are orange and yellow, but their flower and leaf shapes are very different.

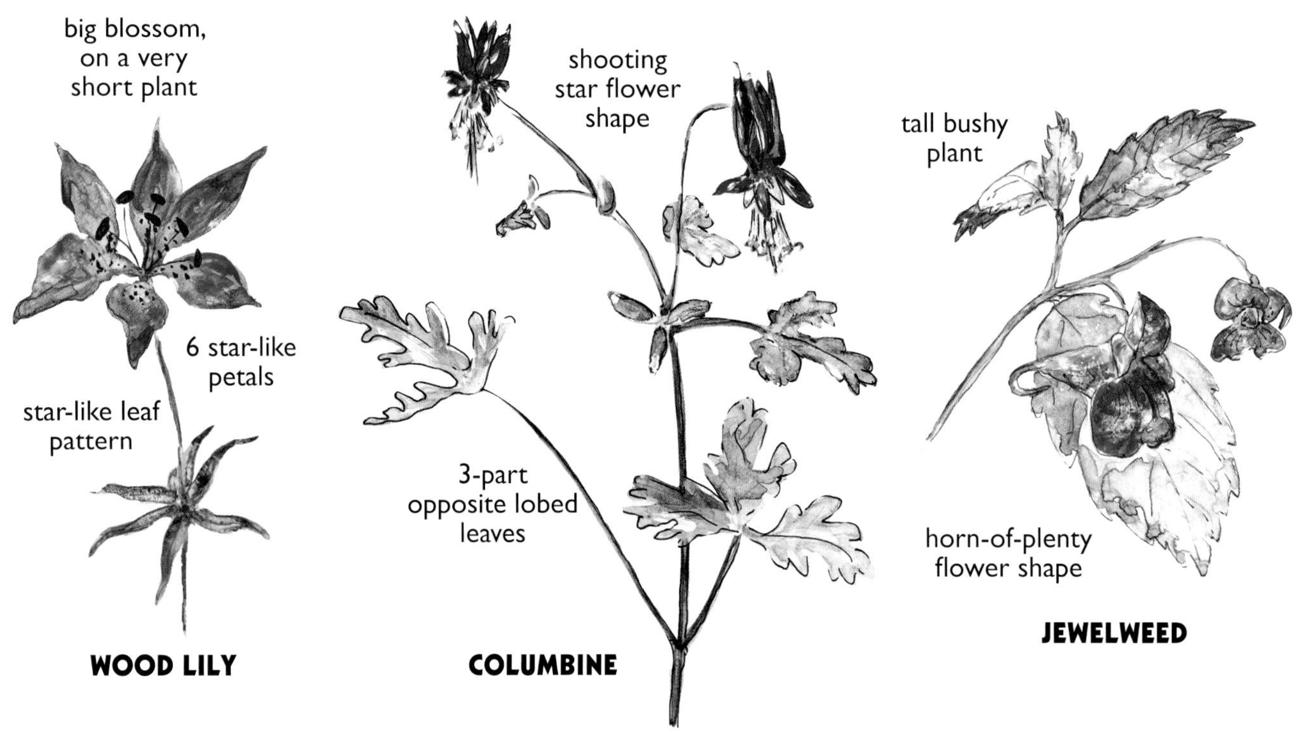
big blossom, on a very short plant
6 star-like petals
star-like leaf pattern
WOOD LILY
shooting star flower shape
3-part opposite lobed leaves
COLUMBINE
tall bushy plant
horn-of-plenty flower shape
JEWELWEED

Mint Hints

Wildflowers with square (4-sided) stems belong to the mint family. Many kinds of mint grow in Michigan woods. Know a mint by its square stem and fragrant, opposite leaves.

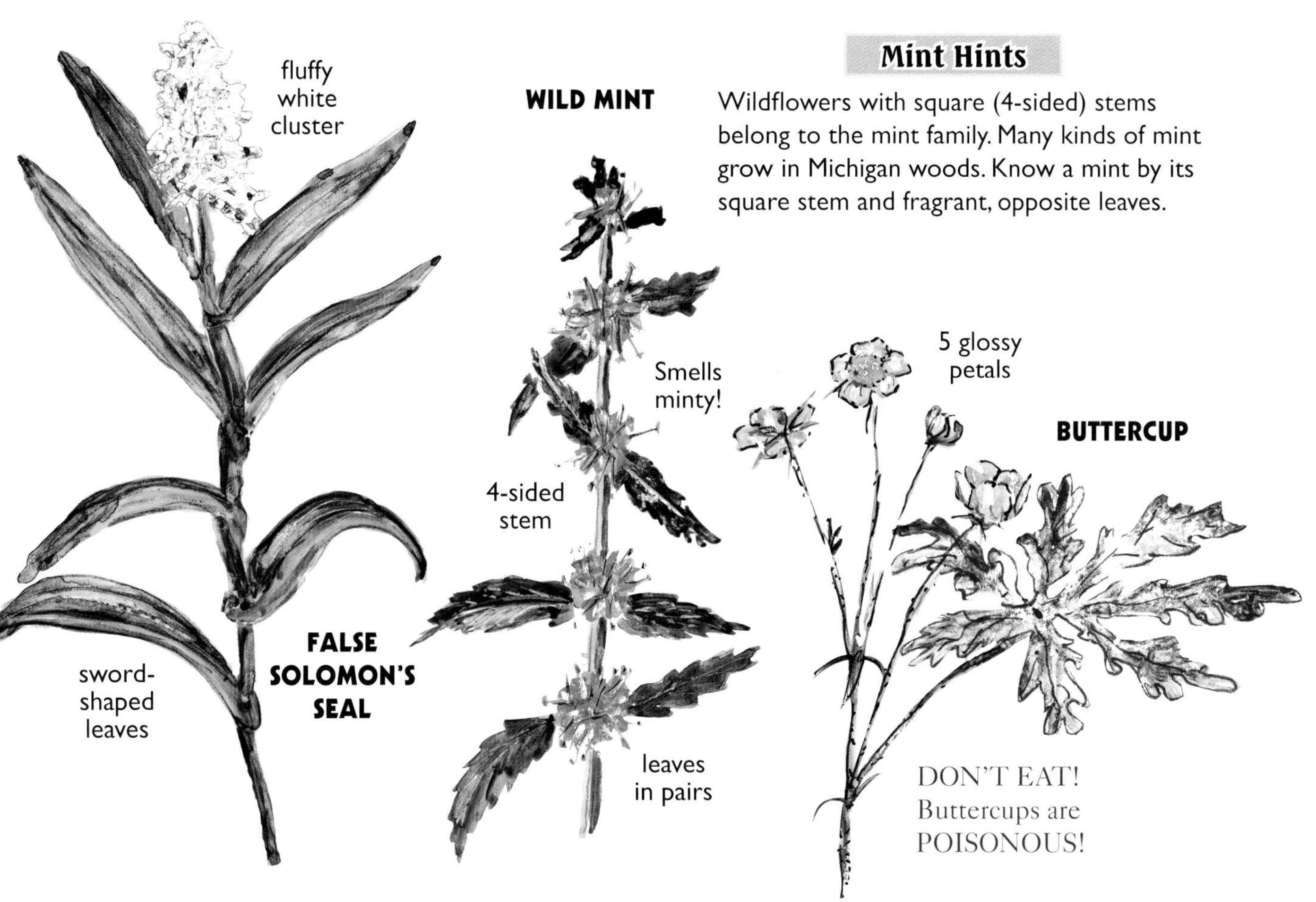
fluffy white cluster
WILD MINT
Smells minty!
4-sided stem
leaves in pairs
5 glossy petals
BUTTERCUP
FALSE SOLOMON'S SEAL
sword-shaped leaves
DON'T EAT! Buttercups are POISONOUS!

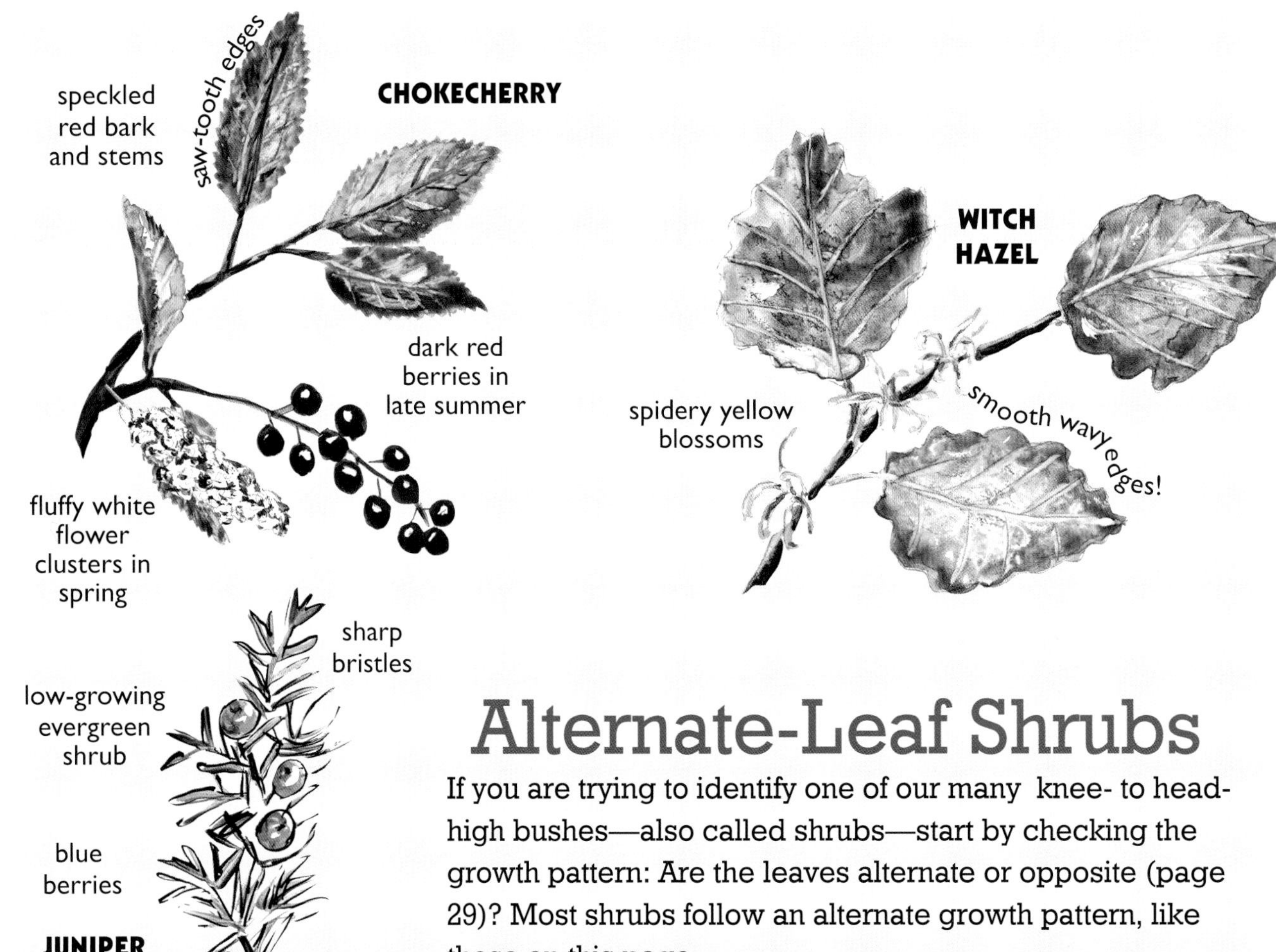
speckled red bark and stems
saw-tooth edges
CHOKECHERRY
dark red berries in late summer
fluffy white flower clusters in spring
WITCH HAZEL
spidery yellow blossoms
smooth wavy edges!
sharp bristles
low-growing evergreen shrub
blue berries
JUNIPER

Alternate-Leaf Shrubs

If you are trying to identify one of our many knee- to head-high bushes—also called shrubs—start by checking the growth pattern: Are the leaves alternate or opposite (page 29)? Most shrubs follow an alternate growth pattern, like those on this page.

Opposite-Leaf Shrubs

Shrubs with opposite leaves are easier to identify, because there are fewer of them. Leaves, branches, and leaf-veins grow in pairs.

The Pair Shrubs

Honeysuckles flowers may be white, orange, pink, red, lavender, yellow, or red, but all of their leaves, blossoms, berries, and branches grow in pairs.

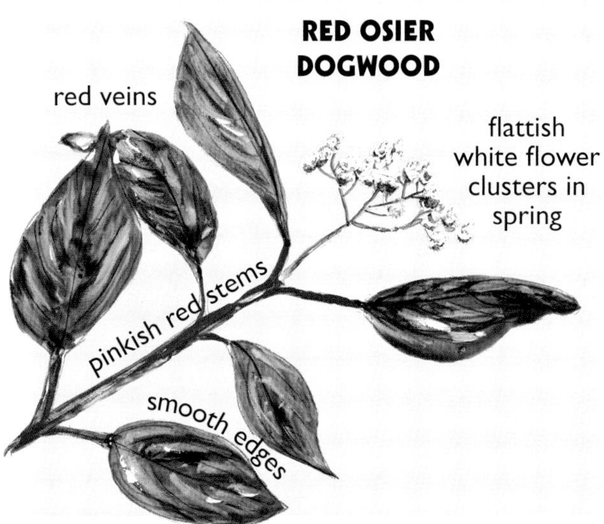

RED OSIER DOGWOOD
red veins
flattish white flower clusters in spring
pinkish red stems
smooth edges

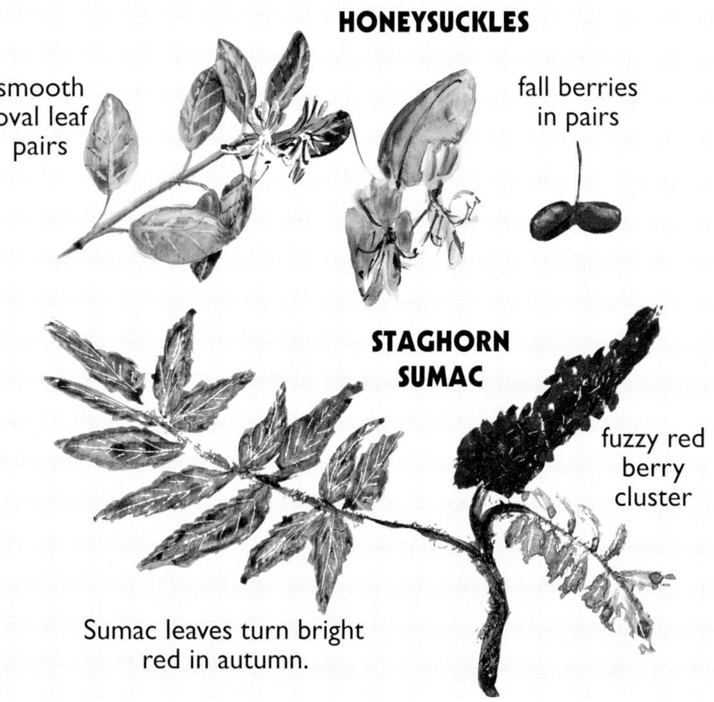

HONEYSUCKLES
smooth oval leaf pairs
fall berries in pairs
STAGHORN SUMAC
fuzzy red berry cluster

Sumac leaves turn bright red in autumn.

Butterflies by Day

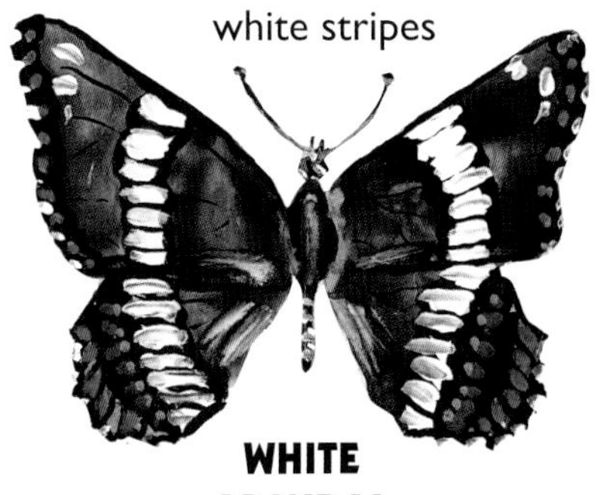
white stripes
WHITE ADMIRAL

BLUE

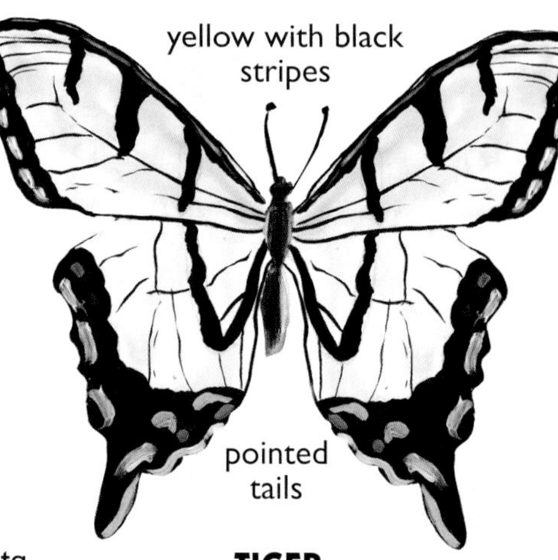
yellow with black stripes
pointed tails
TIGER SWALLOWTAIL

COPPER

A butterfly needs sunshine to warm its body so it can fly. Each of its hair-thin antenna ends in a dot.

lots of freckles
FRITILLARY

mostly purplish brown
MOURNING CLOAK

CECROPIA
HAWK MOTH
TIGER MOTH
LUNA MOTH

Moths at Night

Turn on the porch light after dark to attract night-flying moths. You can tell a moth from a butterfly by its soft, often feathery, antennae and its fat fuzzy body.

Odd Green Plants

DON'T TOUCH!
Poison Ivy can give you a painful rash.

Some plants don't offer many color clues, but these three stand out in other ways. Jack-in-the-pulpit is hardest to find, but Poison Ivy—don't touch!—and Plantain might even grow in your yard.

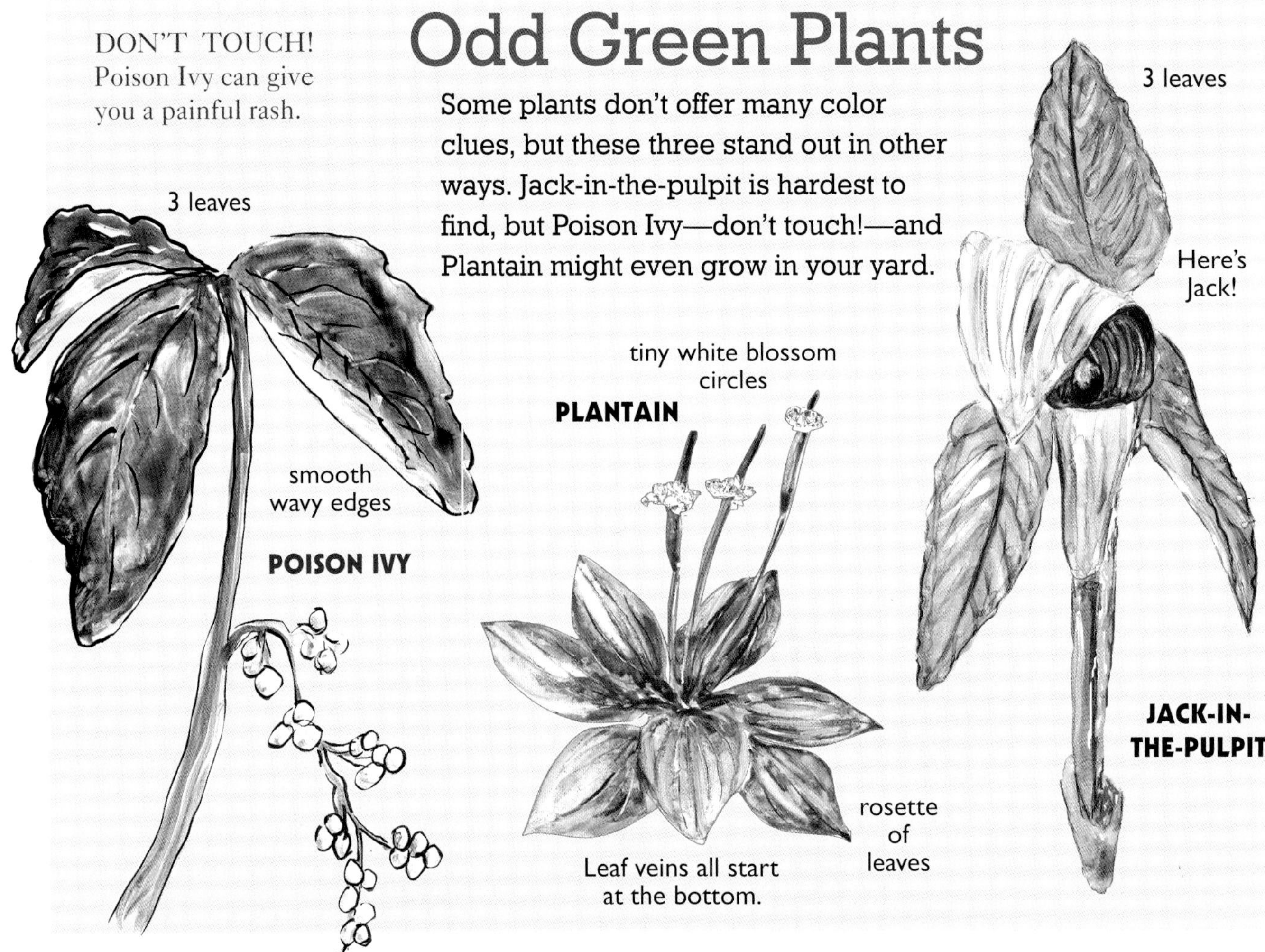
3 leaves
smooth wavy edges
POISON IVY
tiny white blossom circles
PLANTAIN
rosette of leaves
Leaf veins all start at the bottom.
3 leaves
Here's Jack!
JACK-IN-THE-PULPIT

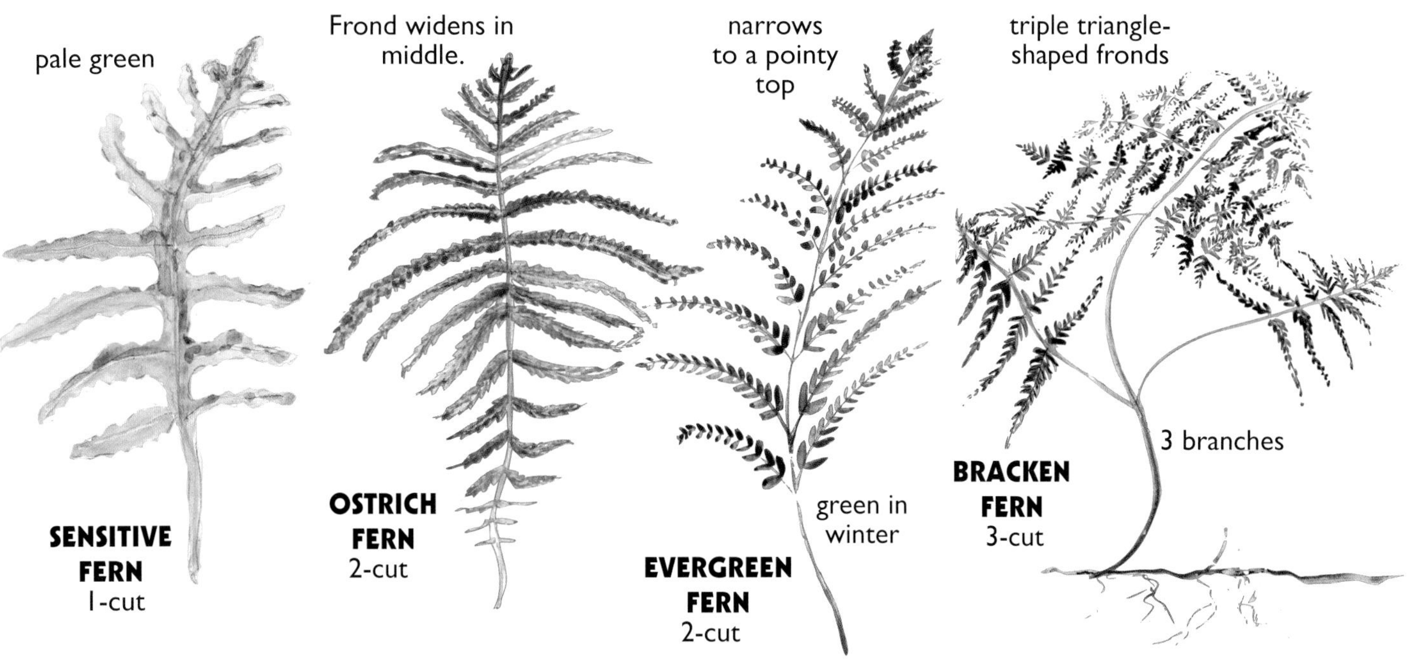
pale green
SENSITIVE FERN
1-cut
Frond widens in middle.
OSTRICH FERN
2-cut
narrows to a pointy top
green in winter
EVERGREEN FERN
2-cut
triple triangle-shaped fronds
3 branches
BRACKEN FERN
3-cut

Fern Frills

Some ferns, like the Bracken Fern, grow waist-high and cover large areas. Others grow here and there and may only reach your knees. The tiny raised dots under fern fronds are called *fruit dots.*

Counting Fern Cuts

The number of times a fern branch divides is called a *cut.* The Sensitive Fern is one-cut. Ostrich and Evergreen Ferns are 2-cut. The Bracken Fern is 3-cut.

Mushrooms All Year

Fungi [FUNG-guy, the scientific word for mushrooms] can be found in all seasons in Michigan. So many species grow in our forests, no one guide book can cover them all. It may be hard to identify mushrooms, but start noticing them. Look at the forest floor, rotten stumps, logs, and tree trunks. How many colors and types you can find?

gills beneath the caps
Grows in bunches, especially on dead oak.

HONEY MUSHROOM
fall

Mushroom Safety

Don't touch any wild mushroom unless someone who knows exactly what it is tells you that it's okay. Most mushrooms are not harmful, but some are deadly poisonous, and others can make you very sick.

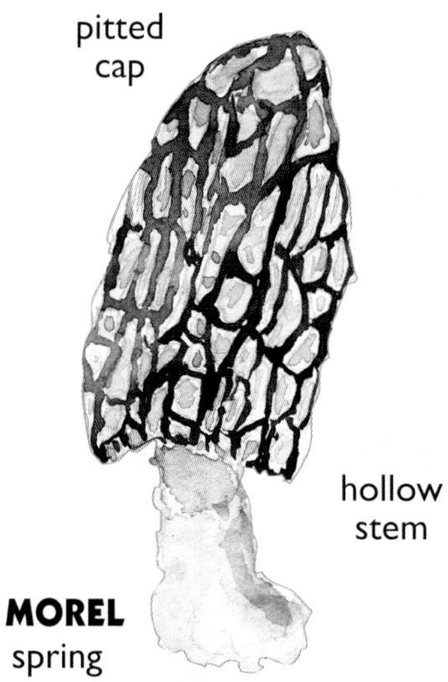
pitted cap
hollow stem

MOREL
spring

Smells like licorice or apricots.

gills underneath the cap

OYSTER
spring

There are many kinds of *boletes*, mushrooms that are spongy under the caps.

spongy underneath

hamburger bun-shaped cap

PALE BOLETE

cottony patches

gills under cap

AMANITA MUSCARIA
summer & fall

cup at bottom of stem

POISONOUS! DON'T TOUCH!

PUFFBALL
summer & fall

Grows on dead Aspen trunks (page 26).

A Puffball may be big as a marble, baseball, or basketball.

Inside is marshmallow white when fresh.

Some Bugs Bite or Sting.

Insects have wings and six legs. *Arachnids* [a-RACK-nids], like ticks and spiders, have eight legs. The insects and arachnids on this page can give you a painful bite. Be extra careful if you are allergic to any of them.

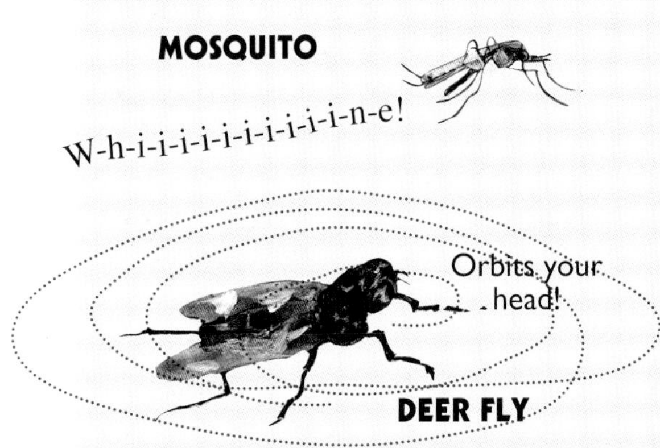
MOSQUITO
W-h-i-i-i-i-i-i-i-i-i-i-n-e!
Orbits your head!
DEER FLY

Lyme Tick?

A bug attached to your skin is a tick. A Wood Tick rarely causes any long-term problems. However, the tiny Deer Tick can carry Lyme disease, a serious illness. To remove a tick, grab it firmly with a pair of tweezers close to the skin and pull straight up. Check Deer Tick bites with a health professional.

fuzzy brown and yellow stripes

HONEY BEE

body stripes

BLACK FLY

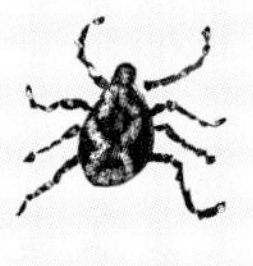

whitish and black

WOOD TICK

All ticks have 8 legs.

Can be as small as a pinhead.

dark red and black

DEER TICK

shiny black and yellow stripes

YELLOW JACKET

LADYBUG

2 or more spots

Some Bugs Don't.

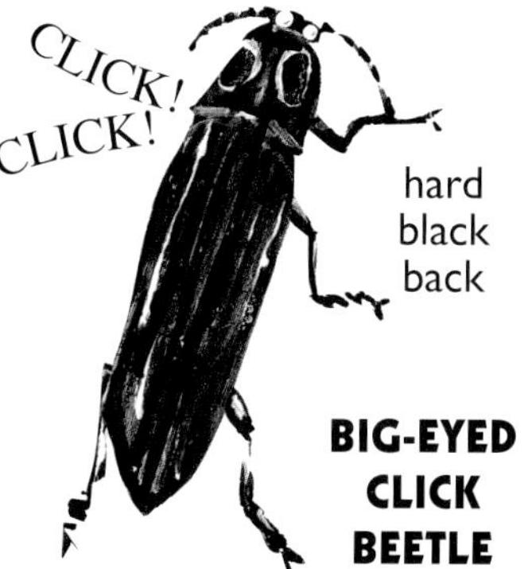
2 big white-rimmed black "eye"spots
CLICK!
CLICK!
hard black back
BIG-EYED CLICK BEETLE

Some of the largest "bugs" will not hurt you. An insect with a hard covering on its "back" is often some kind of beetle. It's fun to look for beetles, which come in many patterns, shapes, colors, and sizes.

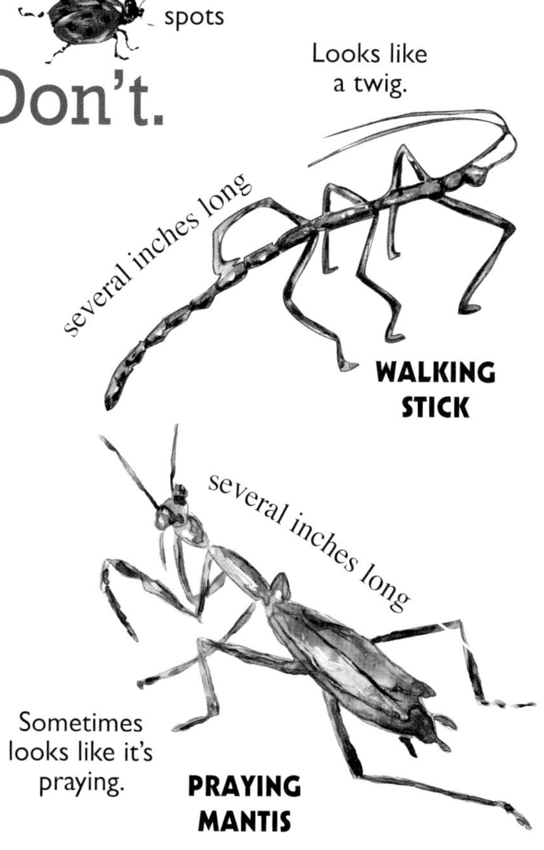
Looks like a twig.
several inches long
WALKING STICK
several inches long
Sometimes looks like it's praying.
PRAYING MANTIS

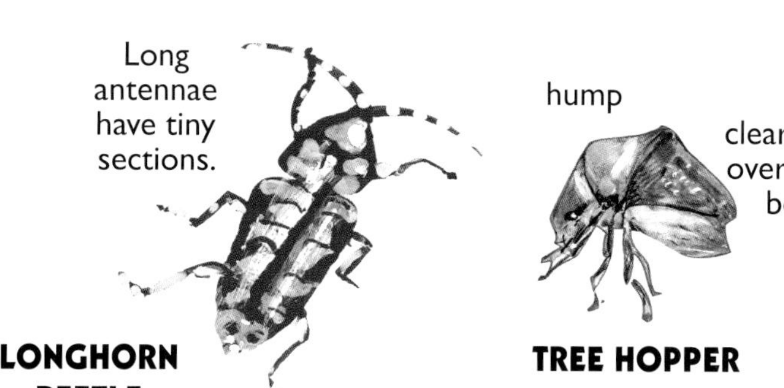
Long antennae have tiny sections.
LONGHORN BEETLE
hump
clear wings over green body
TREE HOPPER

Brambles Scratch!

The forest is full of fruits, especially in late summer and fall. Some are edible—Wild Blackberries and Wild Raspberries are safe to eat—but some berries are poisonous. Never put a berry in your mouth unless someone who knows exactly what it is tells you that it is safe!

red or black ripe fruit
Underside is white.
prickly stems
WILD RASPBERRY

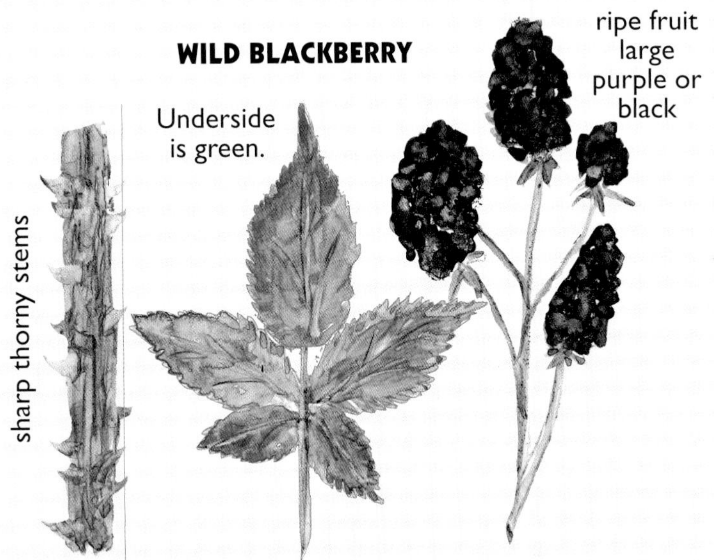
WILD BLACKBERRY
ripe fruit large purple or black
Underside is green.
sharp thorny stems

Brambles

Thorny or prickly vines are called *brambles*. Wild Blackberry brambles have sharp, tooth-shaped thorns. Wild raspberry brambles are covered with needle-like prickles.

These Berries Don't!

These berries are edible and easy to pick—none of the plants has prickles or thorns. Find them growing in patches of low-growing plants, not on vines.

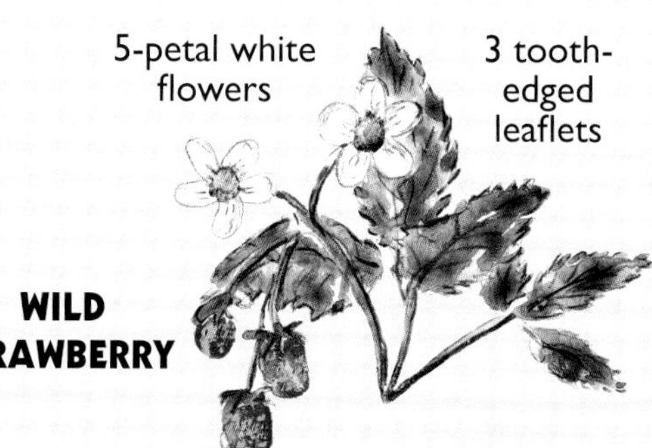
5-petal white flowers
3 tooth-edged leaflets
WILD STRAWBERRY

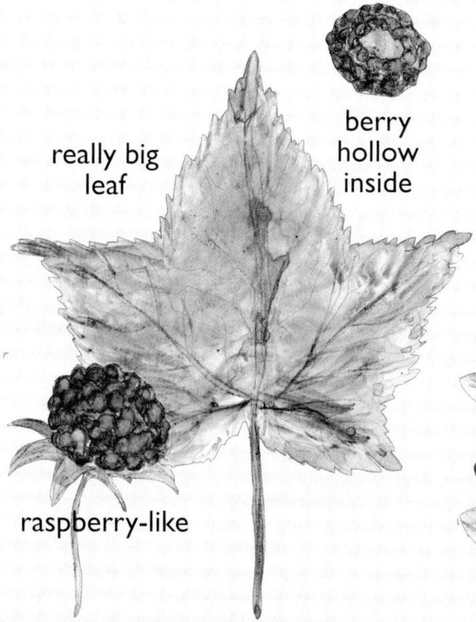

really big leaf

berry hollow inside

raspberry-like

THIMBLEBERRY

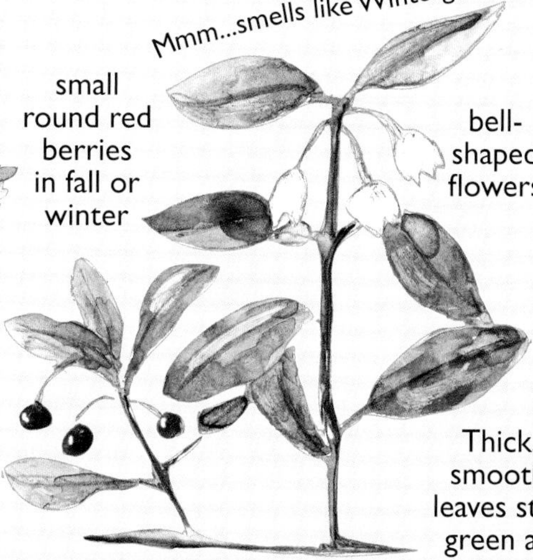

Mmm...smells like Wintergreen gum!

small round red berries in fall or winter

bell-shaped flowers

Thick, smooth leaves stay green all winter.

WINTERGREEN

small smooth leaves

blue or black round berries

pink or white bell-shaped flowers

HUCKLEBERRY

Topical Index

Go to BeaverIslandArts.com to download a checklist.

BIRDS

Bluebird, Eastern, 31
Cardinal, 6
Catbird, 31
Chickadee, 9
Crow, American, 6
Dove, Mourning, 7
Eagle, Bald, 12
Finch, House, 8
Flicker, 11
Goldfinch, 9
Grosbeak, Rose-breasted, 7
Grouse, Ruffed, 14
Hawk, Red-tailed, 12
Jay, Blue, 6
Junco, 11
Nuthatch, White-breasted, 9
Owl, Eastern Screech, 13
Owl, Great Horned, 13
Owl, Snowy, 13
Pheasant, Ring-necked, 14
Robin, 22
Sparrow, House, 8
Swallow, Tree, 30
Thrush, Wood, 31
Titmouse, Tufted, 8
Turkey, Wild (female), inside front cover
Turkey, Wild (male), 14
Vulture, Turkey, 12
Warbler, Yellow, 30
Waxwing, Cedar, 31
Woodpecker, Downy, 10
Woodpecker, Hairy, 10
Woodpecker, Red-headed, 11
Wren, House, 30

INSECTS AND ARACHNIDS

Bee, Honey, 42
Beetle, Big-eyed Click, 43
Beetle, Longhorn, 43
Bumblebee, 22
Butterfly, Blue, 36
Butterfly, Copper, 36
Butterfly, Fritillary, 37
Butterfly, Mourning Cloak, 36
Butterfly, Tiger Swallowtail, 36
Butterfly, White Admiral, 36
Fly, Black, 42
Fly, Deer, 42
Ladybug, 43
Mantis, Praying, 43
Mosquito, 42
Moth, Cecropia, 37
Moth, Hawk, 37
Moth, Luna, 37
Moth, Tiger, 37
Tick, Deer, 42
Tick, Wood, 42
Tree Hopper, 43
Walking Stick, 43
Yellow Jacket, 42

MAMMALS, REPTILES, AND AMPHIBIANS

Bat, Brown, 17
Chipmunk, Eastern, 15
Coyote, 18
Deer, White-tailed, 18
Fox, Red, 18
Hare, Snowshoe, 16
Moose, 18
Opossum, 17
Porcupine, 16
Rabbit, Eastern Cottontail, 16
Raccoon, 17
Rattlesnake, Massasauga, 23
Salamander, Red-bellied, 23
Skunk, 16

Snake, Garter, 23
Snake, Milk, 23
Squirrel, Flying, 17
Squirrel, Gray, 15
Squirrel, Red, 15
Toad, American, 23
Turtle, Box, 23
Woodchuck, 22

MUSHROOMS

Amanita Muscaria, 40
Bolete, Pale, 40
Honey, 41
Morel, 41
Oyster, 40
Puffball, 40

SHRUBS, BRAMBLES, AND BERRIES

Blackberry, Wild, 44
Chokecherry, 34
Dogwood, Red Osier, 35
Honeysuckle, 35
Huckleberry, 45
Raspberry, Wild, 44
Strawberry, Wild, 45
Sumac, Staghorn, 35
Thimbleberry, 45
Wintergreen, 45
Witch Hazel, 34

TREES, EVERGREEN

Cedar, Northern White, 21
Cedar, Red, 21
Fir, Balsam, 20
Hemlock, Eastern, 20
Juniper, 21
Pine, Jack, 19
Pine, Red, 19
Pine, White, 19
Spruce, White, 20

TREES, BROAD-LEAVED

Aspen, Bigtooth, 26
Aspen, Quaking, 26
Basswood, 26
Beech, 27
Birch, White (Paper), 27
Catalpa, 26
Hornbeam, American, 27
Hornbeam, Hop, 27
Leaves, Alternate, 29
Leaves, Opposite, 29
Maple, Red, 28
Maple, Striped (Big Leaf), 28
Maple, Sugar, 28
Oak, Red, 29
Oak, White, 29
Sassafras, 26
Willow, 27

WILDFLOWERS, FERNS, AND GREEN PLANTS

Buttercup, 33
Columbine, 32
Dutchman's Breeches, 24
Fern, Bracken, 39
Fern, Evergreen, 39
Fern, Ostrich, 39
Fern, Sensitive, 39
Hepatica, 25
Ivy, Poison, 38
Jack-in-the-pulpit, 38
Jewelweed, 32
Lily, Wood, 32
May Apple, 25
Mint, Wild, 33
Plantain, 38
Solomon's Seal, False, 33
Spring Beauty, 24
Trillium, 24
Violet, Blue, 25
Violet, Yellow, 25

More Michigan Nature Books by Mary Blocksma

What's on the Beach?
A Great Lakes Treasure Hunt
Go nature treasure-hunting along any of Michigan's 3,000 miles of shoreline. The first book in the What's What Outdoors? series.

Great Lakes Nature:
A Seasonal Guide
Accompany the author on 220 Michigan nature walks from January through December.

To find Mary Blocksma's books and art, or to download a handy checklist for *What's in the Woods?*, go to

BeaverIslandArts.com.

What's in the Woods?

Start treasure-hunting now! How many of the following can you find in the picture?

Birds
Blue Jay
Cardinal
Cedar Waxwing
Chickadee
Crow
Downy Woodpecker
Goldfinch
Great Horned Owl
House Sparrow
Mourning Dove
Red-headed Woodpecker
Red-tailed Hawk
Ring-necked Pheasant
Rose-breasted Grosbeak
Turkey Vulture
White-breasted Nuthatch
Wood Thrush

Mammals
Black Bear
Eastern Chipmunk
Gray Squirrel
Moose
Porcupine
Raccoon
Skunk
White-tailed Deer

Plants and Trees
Buttercup
Columbine
Poison Ivy
Red Oak
Sensitive Fern
Sugar Maple
Violet
White Pine
Wood Lily

Other
Amanita Muscaria
Box Turtle
Earthstars
Mourning Cloak